Seneca Ray Stoddard

West Point military academy

Seneca Ray Stoddard

West Point military academy

ISBN/EAN: 9783742839725

Manufactured in Europe, USA, Canada, Australia, Japa

Cover: Foto ©ninafisch / pixelio.de

Manufactured and distributed by brebook publishing software
(www.brebook.com)

Seneca Ray Stoddard

West Point military academy

WEST POINT

MILITARY ACADEMY.

HART & STODDARD. PUBLISHERS.

PUBLICATION OFFICE,
112 E. 24th St.
NEW YORK

UNITED ⋅ STATES ⋅ MILITARY ⋅ ACADEMY.

WEST POINT

WEST POINT, the site of the United States Military Academy and an important fortress during the revolutionary war, is situated in Orange County, New York, on the western bank of the Hudson about 52 miles from New York City. The Military Academy Buildings and grounds are on a plain about one mile in circuit and containing 160 acres, situated above the river about 175 feet. The historical importance of West Point is too well known to be here noticed. The first provision made for the Military Academy was in 1802, and the State of New York ceded its jurisdiction over the tract of land in 1826.

A more healthy situation could not have been found, and in point of beauty it is unsurpassed. The scenery for miles around is most picturesque and at this point the Hudson caps the climax with its beauty and grandeur. "Cron Nest" and "Mount Independence" stand as mighty and silent sentinels watching over the busy workers on the plain below them. The buildings devoted to the instruction and recreation of the Cadets are spacious and are architectural beauties. The grounds are beautifully laid out and never suffer a want of attention. The Cadet Barracks, Academic Buildings, Library, Superintendent's Office, Mess Hall, Hospital and Riding Hall are the principal buildings. Battery Knox, the Siege and Sea Coast Batteries command the river. West Point already beautiful by nature, and being the recipient of every possible artistic improvement, promises a treat to the visitor in search of one of the most beautiful places on the earth, and to the new cadet a most pleasing place as the scene of his future troubles and pleasures.

PHYSICAL REQUIREMENTS.

No married man can be admitted as a cadet, and should a cadet marry before his graduation, such marriage is considered equivalent to his resignation, and he must leave the Institution accordingly. A Medical Board, composed of three experienced Medical Officers, assembles at West Point at the proper times and examines carefully and thoroughly into the physical qualifications of the candidates for admission. No candidate is admitted into the Military Academy unless in the opinion of this Board, he possesses the requisite physical ability to serve his country in the arduous and laborious station of a military officer not only as the time of his admission, but during his life, and until age shall disable him. The "Oath of Office" administered to him requires that he "serve in the army of the U. S. for 8 years (4 years after graduation unless sooner discharged by competent authority." Resignations are always accepted and a discharge always obtainable, except in time of War, or when the country needs the services of every officer or man; but it costs the Government $5000 to graduate a cadet, and the people have a right to expect some service from him after they have educated him. The age for the admission of cadets to the Academy is between seventeen and twenty-two years; but any person who has served honestly and faithfully not less than one year as an officer or enlisted man in either the regular or volunteer service in the late war for the suppression of the rebellion is eligible for appointment up to the age of twenty-four years. Candidates must be at least five feet in height, and free from any infections or immoral disorder, and generally, from any deformity, disease, or infirmity, which may render them unfit for military service.

MODE OF ENTERING.

Each Congressional District and Territory—also the District of Columbia—is entitled to have one Cadet at the Academy. Ten are also annually appointed *at large*. The appointments (excepting those *at large*) are made by the Secretary of War at the request of the Representative or Delegate in Congress, from the District, or Territory; and the person appointed must be an actual resident of the District, or Territory from which the appointment is made. The appointments *at large* are specially conferred by the President of the United States.

Applications can at any time be made by letter to the Secretary of War, to have the name of the applicant placed upon the register, that it may be furnished to the proper Representative, or Delegate, when a vacancy occurs. The application must exhibit the full name, exact age, and permanent abode of the applicant, with the number of the Congressional District in which his residence is situated. No person who has served in any capacity in the military or naval service of the so-called Confederate States can be appointed.

When practical, appointments are made one year in advance of the date of admission.

Candidates are ordered to report in person to the Superintendent of the Academy, between the 1st and the 20th of June, annually, and are examined immediately after the annual examination of the cadets, and at no other time except when one may be prevented from reporting himself by sickness or some other unavoidable cause. In this case he may be examined in the *last* week of August. A candidate failing to pass the preliminary examination in June should he procure the re-appointment, can have another trial in August. Many succeed the second time who fail the first. The candidate should arrive at West Point on the first day allowed him for reporting, and should report immediately on arriving. He should spend no time at the hotel.

The training, both mental and physical, is remarkably complete.

It is accomplished by a steady and moderate, but never ceasing application.

The Superintendent of the Academy, appointed by the President, is charged with the immediate government of the institution.

The Commandant of Cadets, appointed by the President, is charged with the duty of Instructor in the Tactics of the three arms of the service, and in the rules of Military Police, Discipline and Administration.

The Corps of Cadets is under his immediate command.

Competent officers of the Army, on the application of the Superintendent, are assigned by the Secretary of War to duty at the Military Academy—one as Instructor of Ordnance and Gunnery, one as Instructor of Practical Military Engineering, and such others as may be necessary in the Departments of Instruction, or required to assist the Superintendent in the discharge of his duties.

These, together with the Professors of the Academy, constitute the Academic Board. Officers of the Army are also detailed as Adjutant, Quartermaster and Treasurer of the Academy.

The Cadets are arranged in four distinct classes, corresponding with the four years of study. The Cadets employed on the first year's course constitute the Fourth Class; those on the second year's course the Third Class; those on the third year's course the second class; and those on the fourth year's course the First Class.

The academic duties and exercises commence on the 1st of September, and continue until about the last of June. Examinations of the several classes are held in January and June, and at the former such of the first cadets as are found proficient in studies and have been correct in conduct, are given the particular standing in their class to which their merits entitle them. After either examination, cadets found deficient in conduct or studies are discharged from the Academy, unless for special reasons in each case, the Academic Board should otherwise recommend. Similar examinations are held every January and June during the four years comprising the course of studies.

These examinations are very thorough, and require from the cadet a close

persevering attention to study, without evasion or slighting of any part of the course, as no relaxations of any kind can be made by the examiners.

The studies pursued, and the instruction given, come under the following heads:

1st. Infantry, Artillery, and Cavalry Tactics; and Military Police and Discipline.

2d. Use of the Sword, Bayonet, &c.

3d. Mathematics.

4th. French Language.

5th. Spanish Language.

6th. Drawing.

7th. Chemical Physics; Chemistry; Mineralogy, and Geology.

8th. Natural and Experimental Philosophy.

9th. Ordnance; Gunnery, and the duties of a Military Laboratory.

10th. Ethics; and National, International, and Military Law.

11th. Practical Military Engineering; Military Signaling and Telegraphy.

12th. Military and Civil Engineering, and the Science of War.

Four years are devoted to the course of instruction and suitable parts are assigned to each year.

The classes are divided into Sections suitable for instruction and from time to time cadets are transferred from a higher to a lower section or vice versa, according to their abilities and proficiency. The instruction in each branch of study is proportioned to the capacity of the different sections:—the more profound and difficult subjects and investigations being continued to the higher sections. At the end of each week, the result of the week's progress is recorded and every cadet has an opportunity to determine his relative progress and merit.

The instruction in Infantry, Artillery and Cavalry Tactics, and in the use of the Sword, together with various optional Military Gymnastics afford a proper amount of physical exercise. During the months of July and August, the cadets live in camp, engaged only in military duties and exercises, and receiving practical military instruction.

The following is a list of the hours for daily duties.

Reveille at 5 o'clock, A.M., during the months of May, June, July and August; at 5.30 o'clock, A.M., during the months of April and September; and at 6 o'clock, A.M., during the remainder of the year.

Surgeon's call at half-past 6 o'clock, A.M.

For non-commissioned, the signal for breakfast at 7 o'clock, A.M.

Peep, at half-past seven o'clock, A.M., when in barracks; at 8 o'clock, A.M., when in camp.

Roast Beef, the signal for dinner, at 1 o'clock, P.M.

Retreat, at sunset.

Call to quarters, for study in Barracks, at 30 minutes after return from supper, and on Sunday in addition at 30 minutes after inspection, and at 3 o'clock, P.M. Supper immediately after evening parade, except that at no time shall it be earlier than half-past 5 o'clock, P.M.

Tattoo, at half-past 9 o'clock, P.M.

Taps, the signal to extinguish lights, at 10 o'clock, P.M.

Church-call, half-past 10 o'clock, A.M., on Sundays.

A very strict discipline prevails, which is rigidly enforced.

SOUTH FROM DOCK

WEST POINT FROM THE STEAMBOAT LANDING

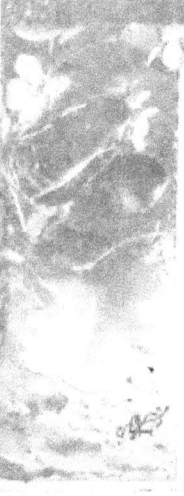

ADMINISTRATION BUILDING

CHAPEL

LIBRARY

LIBRARY

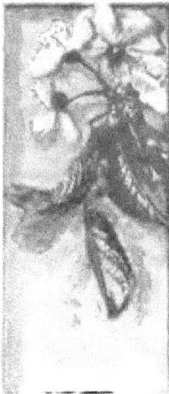

LIBRARY INTERIOR

—THE CHAPEL—

LIBRARY

PHILOSOPHICAL LECTURE ROOM

DRAWING-CLASS-

LABORATORY

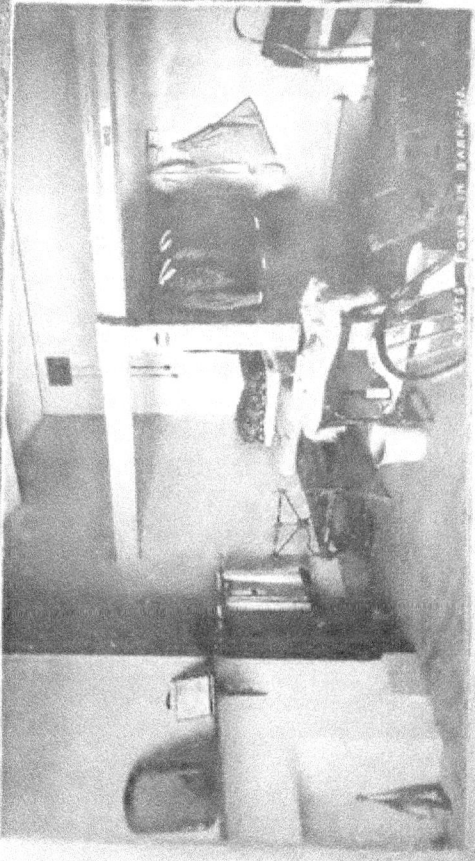

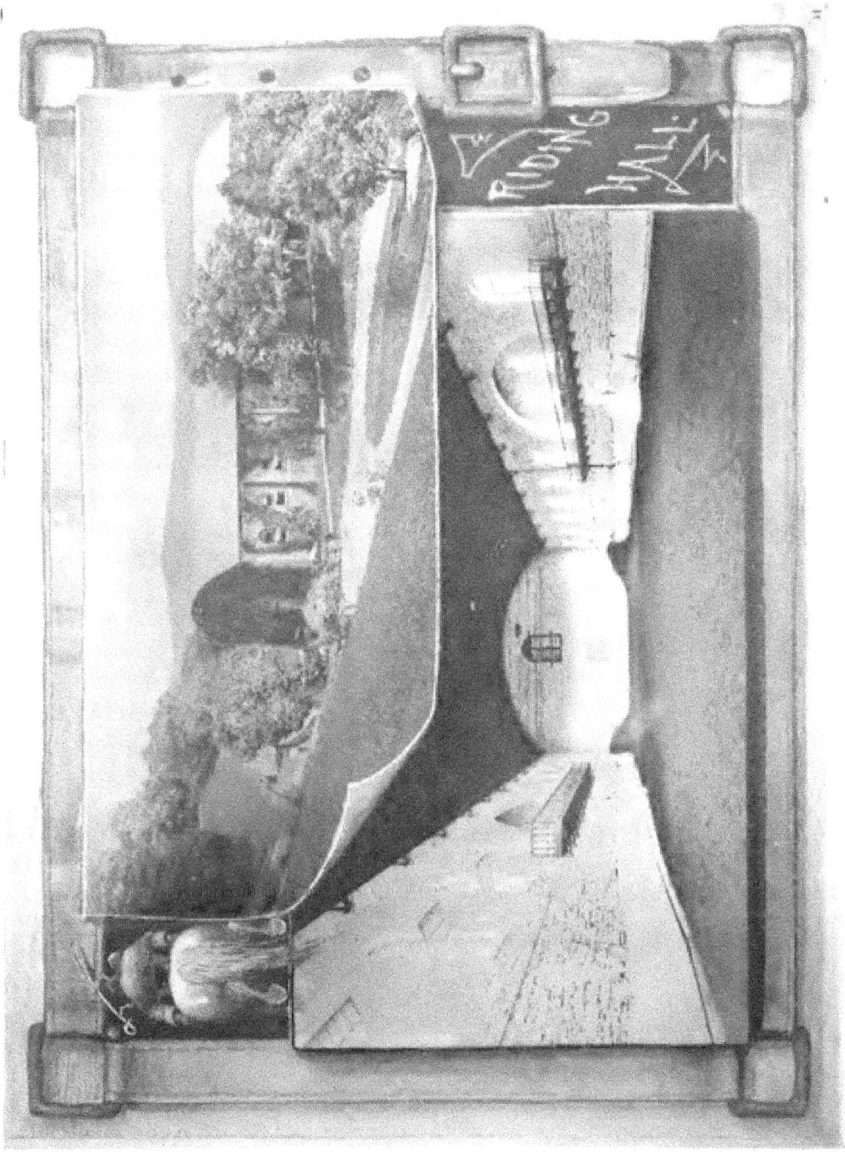

Master of the Hounds

FENCING AT MILL.

GRANT HALL

"AT MESS"

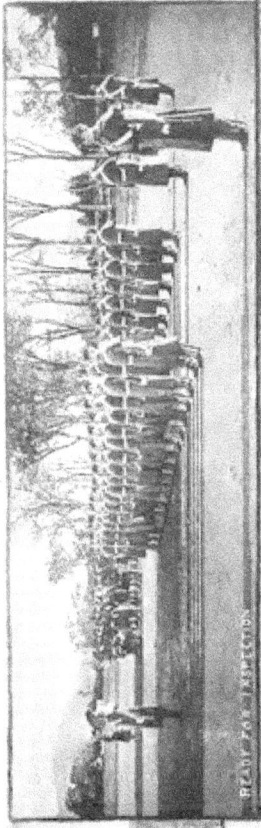

LIGHT · BATTERY · DRILL

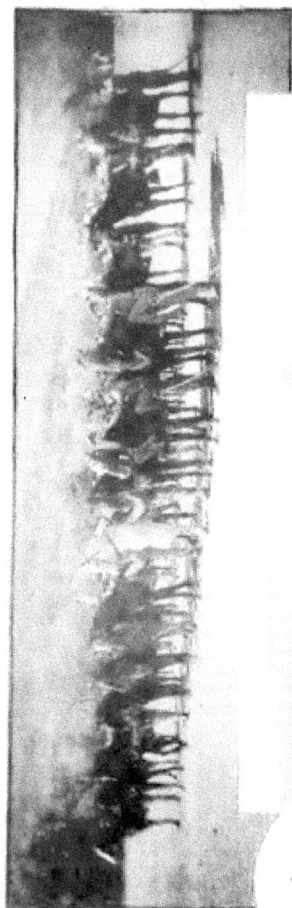

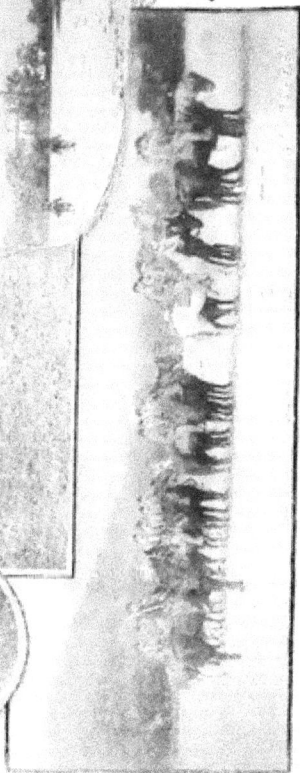

THE CAVALRY PLAIN.

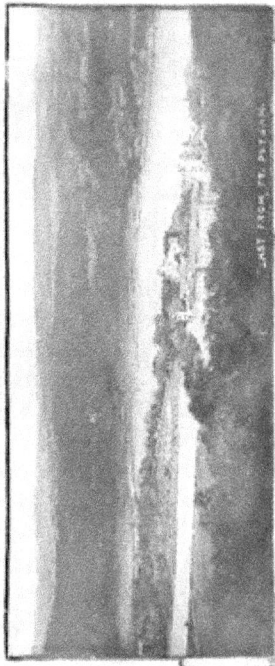

SIEGE BATTERY.

MOUNTING A HEAVY GUN

SEA-COAST BATTERY

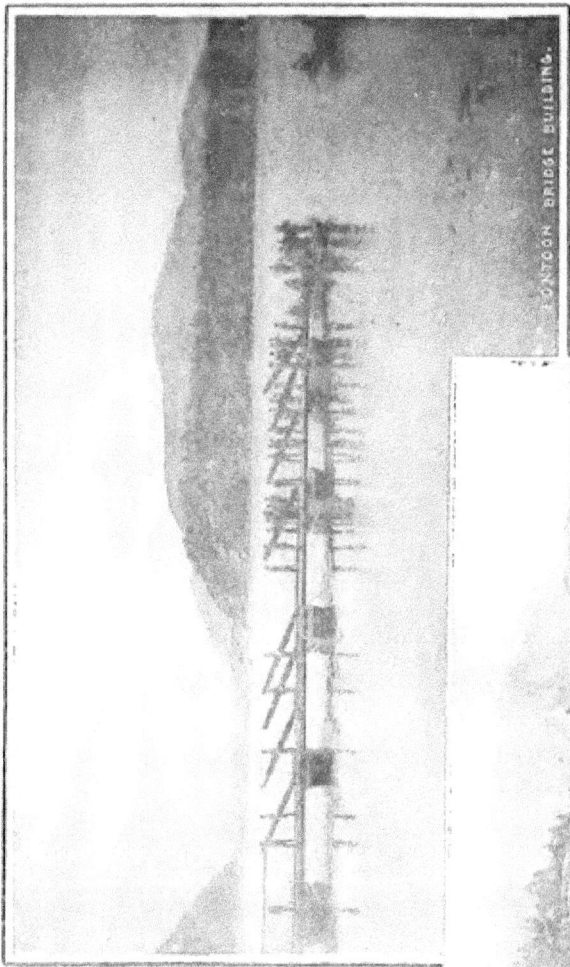

PONTOON BRIDGE BUILDING.

25

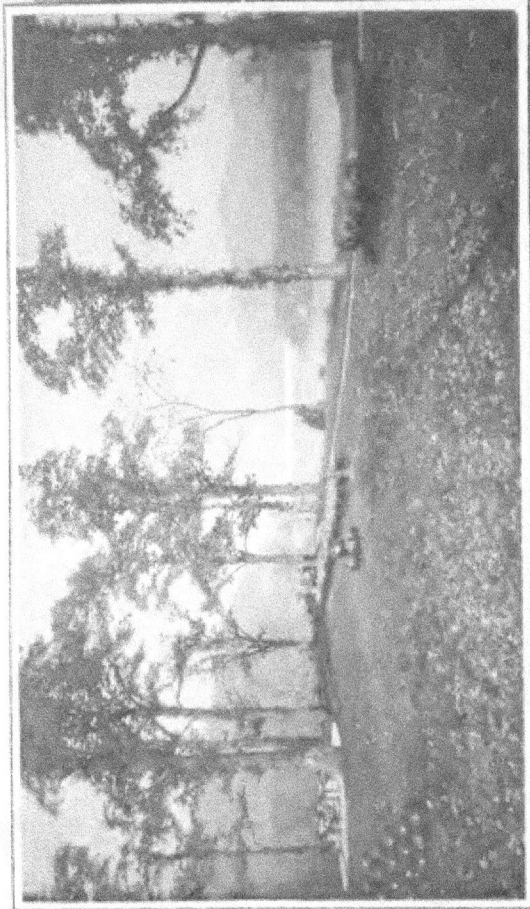

Trophy Room

WEST POINT CEMETERY.

North from Cemetery.

'CADETS' MONUMENT.'

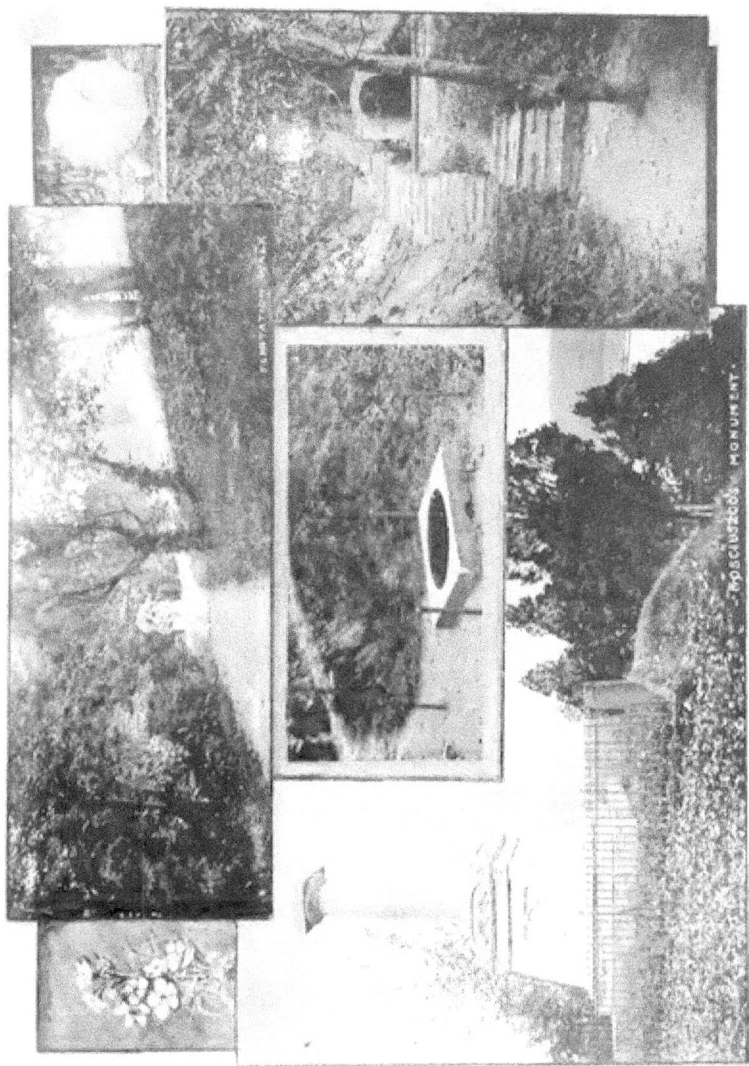

SUNDAY MORNING INSPECTION.

GENERAL PARADE

A COMPANY STREET

OFF DUTY

IN CAMP

"READY"

"AT TAP OF THE DRUM"

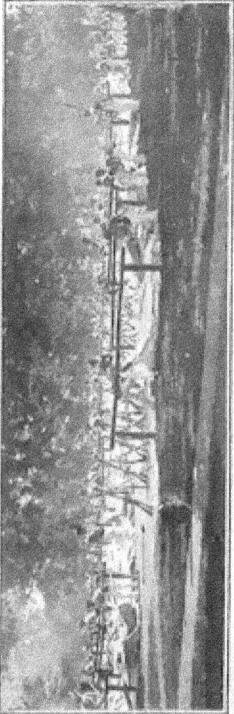

Breaking
Camp

From Camp

to Barracks.

35

"A SATURDAY HALF-HOLIDAY."

MUSICAL CADETS.

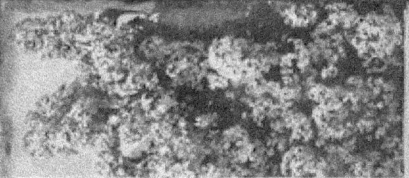

GRENFELL LABORATORY FROM THE WEST.

17

Class of '88

Class of '89

Class of '90